Turning Back the Pages in... Old Carlton

........Compiled by Enid Doona and Paul Tovell

Introduction

According to the trade directories of the nineteenth century, Carlton, or Carlton-in-the-Willows to give it its full title, "is a large and improving township which is built upon an undulating site 3 miles E by N of Nottingham, offering fine prospects of the Vale of Trent from its hills." In 1832 there was a population of 1,704 with the main form of employment being in the lace and hosiery industries. This had grown to 3,973 by 1897 and now stands at 18,116.

In February 2006, a small group of current residents of Carlton came together to begin gathering the contents of this book. Some are directly related to the people listed in those early directories. All have been residents of Carlton for all or most of their lives, and all have stories to tell of Carlton, past and present.

For the purposes of this book we have included the areas of Netherfield and Colwick, as our contributors have tales of work and play which involve these neighbouring places.

Nottinghamshire County Council

Front cover: Carlton Fire Brigade and their new Shand Mason Steam Engine "Progress", c1890

Back cover: South Notts Echo, 1924

Compilers' Note: We have used several documents from Nottinghamshire Archives, and list the reference numbers below in case readers wish to examine them further:

SBX 314/5/1 – Speech Day (p5)   DD H169/126 – Inquisition (p15)
DD 2297/3/1 – Lawrence AGM (p15)   SL 30/5/1 – School Log Book (p39)

Some of the pictures in this book have been reproduced courtesy of Picture the Past, a non-profit making project that makes historic images from the library and museum collections of Derby, Derbyshire, Nottingham and Nottinghamshire, freely available at the click of a button to anyone with access to the Internet, anywhere in the world. See thousands more pictures like this at www.picturethepast.org.uk

© 2007 Nottinghamshire County Council

ISBN 978-0-902751-57-6

Carlton Board School, c1910

This is an outside view of the school from Burton Road. The Carlton Board School opened in 1878, accommodating 500 children who all paid two pence per week to attend. These schools were run by school boards elected by the ratepayers. In 1902, the Education Act swept away the Board Schools, and public education passed into the hands of the council. This school later became the first Carlton Central Primary School, which lasted until the 1960s before subsidence led to its demolition.

Carlton National School, 1902

This photograph shows some of the many children who later went off to fight in the First World War. Standing in the second row from the front on the left of the photograph are Harry and Cyril Ward, born in 1896 and 1897 respectively, who were both killed in the war within three weeks of each other. On the top row, the third figure from the left is Miss Challonds, the headmistress.

Carlton National School, c1900

This school opened in 1869, with Henry Madden as the first headteacher.

St Paul's Church School, 1973

This is the same school, known as St Paul's by now. It stood opposite the church, but has since been demolished. The teachers were memorable figures: *"Reginald 'Slogger' Bond (headteacher from 1941 to 1946) got his name from caning a lot of the boys, whereas Mr Pykett was known for his ultra-modern rolling blackboard in the 1950s."* The other headteachers were William Collishaw, John Raine, F. Melbourne, Idris Richards and Gerry Price: not many for a school that lasted 114 years. It eventually closed in 1983.

Station Road School, c1946

This girls' school was founded in 1910. *"On Speech Day (see programme on the left), prizes were given to girls that had done well during the year. The ceremony was held at the local cinema (the Ritz) on Burton Road. During one memorable wartime lunch break a single German plane came over, machine-gunning Station Road. The girls dashed to the air raid shelters under the playing field, and thankfully there were no casualties."* This is a photograph of an education day display in about 1946, where the girls demonstrated their dancing skills. A sizeable audience is visible at the edge of the playground.

Station Road School Speech Day, 1948

St John's School, Colwick, 1914

"Mr Brown started as head of the old Colwick School as it is on this photograph. He was still headmaster when the new school was built to replace it. After the new school burnt down, he was yet again the head of the third school, all on the same site." This picture was taken on Empire Day, which was a special day for all schools. The teacher on the right is ironically named Mr Peace.

St John's School, Colwick, 1914

This view inside the schoolroom shows the old screen dividing two rooms. This picture was also taken on Empire Day, 1914. The school must have hired an official photographer especially to commemorate the celebrations – no doubt a rare treat for the children.

Old Screen Open Empire Day 1914

(215) ASHWELL ST. C.C. SCHOOLS, NETHERFIELD

Ashwell Street School, Netherfield, 1906-07

This was the original Netherfield Board School, founded in 1894 to serve the rapidly expanding railway village. The juniors inhabited the building on the left of this photograph, while the infants occupied the right-hand one. The house to the left of the school was the caretaker's or headteacher's house.

"Two of the teachers in the late 1930s were Miss Wells and Miss Wayne, both typical 'old maid' elderly teachers, and both shared a house together."

School Attendance Certificate, 1896

CARLTON NATIONAL SCHOOL.

.... has attended ....

times out of a possible ....*during Quarter*

ending ....

1896.

The Government Report for 1896 is as follows :—"This is a very good School and the Singing is excellent." Full grant earned.

The "Excellent" Merit Mark and Grant were received for the Drawing

Progress is only possible with Regular Attendance.

NEVER ABSENT.

In 1891, '92, '93, '94, '95, & '96. Wm. Brearnsley (received a Silver Watch).

In 1893, '94, '95, & '96.—Wm. Seale.

In 1894, '95, & '96.—M. Stirring, T. Yarwood, Walter Croshaw, Wm. Croshaw, Ada Adkin, B. Smedley, A. Priest.

In 1895 & '96.—Wm. Scott, O. Hoy, N. Oakland, L. Oakland.

In 1896.—Wm. Miles, Ernest Goddard, John Adkin, Geo. Topham, Fdk. Pearson, Ch. Toebr, Eva Glazer, Maud Oakland, Jos. Oakland, Fred. Robinson, Geo. Cant, Thos. Seale, D. Hill, Geo. Varnam, Albert Piggott, A. Swinscoe, Hy. Rodinson, Thos. Cant, Thos. Howarth, Geo. Tivey, Wm. Marriott, T. G. Musson, Fre. Butcher, Ada Shalu, Ed. Pearson.

The present Corresponding Manager is Rev. F. J. Perry, the Rector of Carlton.

HEAD MASTER   -   -   -   MR. JOHN RAINE.

Chandos Street School, c1950s

In 1906, the boys from Ashwell Street School split off from the girls, forming a boys' school known as Chandos Street School. This could take 420 boys. During the 1940s, the school gardens stretched alongside the Midland railway line on Chandos Street. The teachers may have suffered from the noise of the nearby trains: *"Miss Ribchester, who was deaf, was perfectly able to lip-read the Ministry of Information films she screened, but was unable to tell whether her children were being suitably quiet until the headteacher complained about the noise."* The other teachers pictured here include Mr Marsh (back row, second from left), Mr Richards (back row, third from left), Mr Parks (front row, third from left) and Mr Grady (front row, second from left).

Chandos Street School, c1930

This is a school class from the 1930s. The teacher, Mr Les Banham, is on the back row.

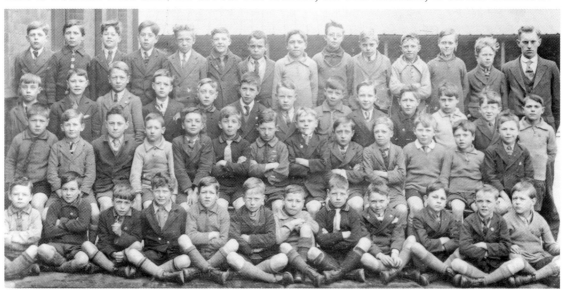

Netherfield Infants' School Staff, 1960s

On the back row (left to right) are: Mrs D. Stirland (Secretary), Mrs M. Croft, Mrs B. Stainforth and Miss M. Groves (Deputy Head). On the front row are: Mrs M. Wilson, Mrs M. Boston, Miss C. S. Johnson (Head), Mrs E. Starbuck, and Mrs N. Foster.

Jimmy Savile at Netherfield Infants' School, 1980s

Jimmy Savile was a regular visitor to Netherfield Infants' School for many years in the 1970s and 1980s. *"He used to stay in nearby Gunthorpe on a Saturday night and would attend a gala dinner, wearing something outrageous. Then he would come to the school for a couple of hours on the Sunday morning, occasionally even broadcasting his radio programme from there. Later, he would do a 6 mile run with some teenagers, and finish the weekend by giving the sermon in Holme Pierrepont parish church."*

St Paul's Church, c1900

"I remember Mr Young the Verger living in the old house next to the school. He was there all my growing-up years and was waiting to bully me down the aisle when I got married. I remember feeling panicky and he told me to pull myself together, which was probably just the push I needed at the time. I have some newspaper cuttings entitled "Italian Basilica-style for Earl" telling me a little bit about the history of the church, with a very nice picture of the inside and Jack McGinley banking on God's cash to boost the fund for the alterations." The church was built in two parts, between 1885 and 1891.

St Paul's Church Hall, 1975

"Inside these buildings were the parish rooms. There was a big hall on the first floor with a wooden spiral staircase, where the children were allowed to see old films at Christmas, such as Laurel and Hardy. The church hall was also used for plays, and the local Brownies met there." These buildings have now disappeared.

St Paul's Bible Class, 1930

This cheery group posing on a bench includes the Reverend Fisher Ferguson, who was the rector (second from the left in the second row) and to his left, Mr Reavill, the class leader.

St Paul's Choir, 1948

"I joined the choir at St Paul's when I was 11 as a boy soprano. It was great, we were all such good friends. Our choir-master was S. J. Burdett, a kindly patient man, but an excellent teacher and organist. We felt very proud when we walked down the church singing the recessional hymn at the end of the service and getting kindly smiles from the congregation. One of my cherished memories is of the month-end. We received our "wages" – sixpence each. So after practices, we lads "high tailed" it to Amy's chip shop on Main Street to buy our own chips!"

Church Choir Procession, Carlton Cemetery, 1910s

"I attended St Paul's School across the road from the church, and we used to visit the church quite often in the 1940s. We would crocodile across to church for Harvest Festivals and Ascension Day services and during the school year there were other religious visits. There was a band made up of scouts, guides, and cubs. Every Sunday morning they would parade around Carlton which caused great excitement, especially the man with the big drum and leopard-skins plus the trumpet. I joined the brownies just to follow the band."

Sacred Heart of Jesus Roman Catholic Church

After nine years of fundraising, the foundation stone of the new church was laid by Bishop Dunn in 1930 and the first Mass celebrated on 27th January 1931. After the service in the church, Father Toomey, Parish priest throughout this period, the Bishop  and distinguished guests enjoyed a meal of oxtail soup, lemon sole, roast sirloin of beef or leg of lamb followed by apple tart and cream. The church was later consecrated by Bishop Edward Ellis on 21st May 1945. The original church, built in 1877, became the parish hall.

St Paul's Girl Guides, 1959

The captain on the left of this group of girl guides is their leader, Miss Christine Johnson.

Main Street Baptist Church, 1900

The Baptists built their first church in 1823 in what is now known as Burton Road, next door to the Black's Head pub. By 1899 their congregations were spilling out of the premises, with 19 baptisms that year. So a new site was acquired in Urban Road (now Station Road), and a building designed by Richard Whitbread to seat 450 worshippers. It cost £2,866, and was opened on 8th April 1901. This photograph of the old church was taken just before the move. The date-stone is engraved "General Baptist Chapel, 1844".

Main Street Methodist Church, 2006

Carlton Methodists have met to worship on the same spot on Carlton Hill since 1854. The present church building was opened in 1898, and has retained the name "Main

Street" despite the road being re-named Carlton Hill in 1951. By 1933, the two houses on Cromwell Street, next to Main Street Church, had been demolished to make room to build a caretaker's house at a cost of £450. The caretaker, Mr Wright, paid 8 shillings and sixpence per week rent, and received one guinea per week in wages.

**Lawrence Factory
AGM, 1895**

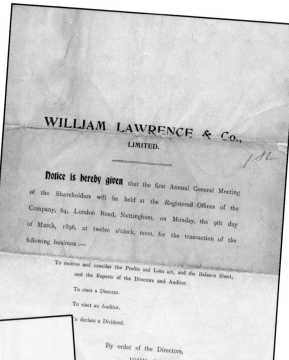

WILLIAM LAWRENCE & Co.,
LIMITED.

Notice is hereby given that the first Annual General Meeting
of the Shareholders will be held at the Registered Offices of the
Company, 64, London Road, Nottingham, on Monday, the 9th day
of March, 1896, at twelve o'clock, noon, for the transaction of the
following business :—

To receive and consider the Profits and Loss a/c, and the Balance Sheet,
and the Reports of the Directors and Auditor.

To elect a Director.

To elect an Auditor.

To declare a Dividend.

By order of the Directors,

JOHN G. STEPHENSON,
Secretary.

AD, NOTTINGHAM,
RUARY, 1896.

**Featherstone
Inquisition, 1898**

Seniority List, Colwick Loco Works, 1968-69

Displayed on the wall in a glass notice case at Colwick Loco Works was a seniority list. It had everyone's start dates on it, and so must have been frequently updated. The one in this photograph dates from the late 1960s, when the Works was about to shut down. It was rescued from the works by Mr Cockayne, whose name appears towards the bottom of the right-hand column. He is pictured holding it below.

N.		S.D.
	D.M.	7.10...
Clark	P.	7.10.4
Groves	L.W.	14.10.46
Tacey	R.	14.10.46
Ringham	J.D.	21.10.46
	A.E.	16.12.46
Meredith	E.	3.2.47
Peck	J.V.	10.3.47
Sharpe	C.N.	27.5.47
Button	P.	24.6.47
As nall	J.	7.7.47
Daykin	D.W.	21.7.47
Groves	D.A.	1.9.47
Kitchener	J.W.	22.9.47
Jones	W.	30.12.47
Wright	C.G.	2.2.48
Blount	H.	16.2.48
Young	P.	1.3.48
Austin	B.C.	3.5.48
Harvey	R.L.	24.5.48
Perry	A.T.	24.5.48
Ell	J.K.	9.6.4
Harris	N.W.	9.8.43
Epton	A.P.	20.9.48
Grocock	E.	10.1.49
Cumberpatch	L.	4.7.49
Wilson	R.A.	1.5.50
Cockayne	R.	12.6.50
Peet	C.R.	1.8.50

Mr Cockayne with the Seniority List, 2006

Enginemen's Roster, Colwick Loco Works, 1960s

These are rosters from the 1960s, showing what jobs the enginemen were doing. *"A driver and a fireman would work the same job, or train route, all week, and would stick together as a team for 4-5 months. The trains were quite slow: 60 wagons of coal would limit your speed to about 25mph, meaning it took a long time to get anywhere. There were 24 jobs altogether, going out to iron ore mines, and places as far as March in Cambridgeshire, and Wellingborough in Northants. After clocking on, you would prepare your engine which might take an hour, journey down for several hours, then wait to take the empty wagons back again. At least at that speed, there were no crashes."*

Driver	Fireman	SUNDAY		MONDAY	
		On Duty	Turn/ Dia. No.	On Duty	Turn/ Dia. No.
Holford	D Wakefield	Toton		09.25	92
Mason	M Collier	Chaddesden		2155	39 180
G Wright	G Bakewell	Bel Stanton		0825	89
R Beavers	S Miller	Wellingboro		19.08	112
Catling	J Yargett	Gedling		R	D
Flowers	T Rockley SD	Toneden Rd		20.15	37
J Bathwell	D Savage	Nottm NS		0510	140
C Boultby	W Bell	Linby		12.25	135
T James	R Sutton	R	R	R	D
E Ogden	B Greenfield	Northampton March BOSTON		17.23	106
L Salthern	K Wilson	Linby		0630	134
R Preston	H Heyland	Wellingboro		22.33	118
J Watson	J Swann	Chaddesden		1155	95
R Bromwich	D Hughes	Bel Stanton		15.15	101
J Purdy	G Thompson	Hucknall		04.55	130
R Herbert	R B Davies	Northampton TSH BOSTON MNE		1645	103

Colwick Sidings, 1923

This is a coal stage, showing an engine being filled with coal in Colwick sidings.

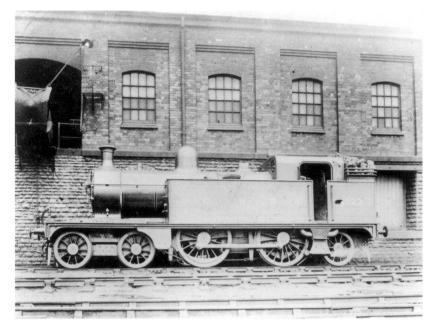

Colwick Loco Works, c1900s

Colwick Loco Works had a large mess due to the number of people that worked there. It was usually a crowded place: *"If anyone mashed a cup of tea it would vanish within seconds. Except for a driver named Bernard Kingston who would stir his tea with his false teeth and then invite everyone to help themselves."*

Colwick Engine Cleaners, 1930

On the left is Frank Newham, Syd Gee is in the centre, and George Allen is on the right.

Colwick Sidings, 1960s

The staff line-up here at Colwick sidings is Ernie Yardley, Inspector Skinner from London, E. J. "Mick" Tyler (who was always being told what to do) and George Allen (who lived to 100). In the background is a new brush diesel, which hauled wagons up and down on a goods line.

Gell's Coal Merchants, c1890s

"All coal merchants had their own site, where they had coal delivered directly from the pit. There were plenty of pits around, producing different grades of coal such as Top Brights, Top Hard, High Hazel, and Cobbles. There were many merchants in the Carlton area, including: Matty Man (Netherfield), Trumans (Netherfield), Leapers (Foxhill Road), Drings (Gladstone Street), Fred Young (Station Road), Oldhams (Deep Furrow Avenue), Harry Hawkins (Beck Street), Sam Felstead (Carlton Hill), and Jackie Redall." This picture shows the entrance to one of the merchants' yards right by the railway line.

Carlton Fire Brigade, 1909

"My mother lived at the bottom house on Wallace Avenue (opposite the current fire station) as a child. She said that as children, they would hear the bells ringing at the fire station and would rush out to watch as the firemen had to run to the field at the back of it. There they would have to catch the horses and harness them to the fire engine before 'racing' off down the road." Here they are, all assembled and ready for action in 1909.

Lawrence's Factory, Colwick, 1977

This was a big furniture factory in Colwick, built in 1899 on what is now Hotspur Road. *"Lots of Carlton people worked here – it was the second biggest employer in the area, after the railways. During the war, aeroplanes were made here. After the demolition of the factory, the new road on the site was named after one of the planes."*

Bourne's Factory Colwick, c1909

In the background of this photograph, you can see the high chimney of Bourne's Factory. This is where cotton was spun. It was delivered in its raw state from Lancashire, and put onto bobbins within these walls. Then it would be taken on to the nearby framework knitters' workshops, one of the

big industries in old Carlton. In 1812 Nottingham alone had 2,000 frames. But the hours were long in this domestic industry (up to 14 hours per day depending on daylight), the conditions were poor, and the wages were low, especially when you had to pay for the hire of your frame. By the time of this photograph, the industry was almost extinguished due to the rise of steam power.

Mar Hill Brewery and Maltings, 1985

"The Ilkeston Hosiery Company came to Carlton's Mar Hill Road site in the 1960s. At that time, Mr Cornish was the Assistant Manager, Mr Goodwin was the Manager, Sam Dextor was the Foreman, and Annie was Women's Foreman. The company finished nylon stockings, but the old brewery was previously used in the 1930s as a dye house, as there was a well underneath."

Stead's Coachbuilders, 1977

Here on Station Road, men used to heat the iron rims, and then fitted them to the wooden wheels using buckets of water to shrink the iron. The workshop has since been demolished and Stead Close built in its place.

Cope's Butchers, Netherfield, 1903

The sign hanging around the left hand pig's neck says that the pig came 3rd in the Christmas Fat Stock Competition, Tuesday 13th December 1903. This is a traditional turn-of-the-century butcher's shop in Netherfield. On either side of the pigs are huge sides of beef and oxtails, whilst above there are shoulders and legs of lamb.

Mr Aslin, 1920s

John Aslin was a Carlton butcher with a tiny shop on Main Street. In this photograph he is feeding birds in an orchard believed to have been at the top of Carlisle Road. When he died his daughter Nelly, who worked with him, ran the shop. The shop is now disused and boarded-up, and Nelly has retired to Hucknall.

Foxhill Close, Carlton Hill, 1975

There were many butchers in the Carlton area at one time. When Joe Smith set up his shop at 30 Carlton Hill, there were 12 small butchers' shops in the pictured area. By the 1980s his was the only one left, as all the others had been replaced by Tesco's meat department. Joe Smith killed both for his shop and for Atkins butchers. The centre house in this photograph belonged to the Tipler sisters, and you can also see Vickerstaffs, Rex Robinson bikes, and Mrs Shelton's haberdashery. The woodyard behind belonged to Ernest King, the brother of Reg, the famous boxing promoter.

Carlton Hill, 1930s

"Under the canopy was my first shop in Carlton: Spurr's Grocers. I drove the van to deliver groceries. We sold bird seed and tinned goods as well as groceries. People were very trusting – they would take their family allowance from the post office and bring it straight to us and leave it with us all week, coming in to collect their loaf of bread every day. People used to knock on the back door and wake us up saying "Have you anything for my sandwich?" and we'd get up and serve them! We were lucky, too: the shop had a bath, and 3 upstairs rooms. The shop had a bit of a colourful history: the person who had the grocers before us had murdered his wife in the back of the shop, after a mental breakdown when he lost all his ration coupons."

Hannam's Ironmongers, Carlton Hill, 1950s

"There were many local shops on Carlton Hill in the 1950s. The off-licence on Foxhill Road sold everything from a bundle of sticks for the fire to Indian brandy for stomach ache, besides the usual draught beer sold in customers' jugs or bottles. Meanwhile Mrs Thorpe down the road sold sweets, Tizer, Dandelion and Burdock and ice cream. She also had a large grey parrot in her back room that used to shout out when anyone entered the shop."

Carlton Hill, 1950s

Before the development of Tesco's in the 1980s, local food stores included Baggaley the butcher: a very large shop where you could fetch potted meat and tripe. *"All the shops in this area faced the threat of a long-running rumour that one or both sides of the road were to be pulled down to make room for an 80-feet wide dual carriageway. A further rumour was that the entire area from Post Office Square to the east side of Manor Road was to be demolished and replaced by a civic centre. This was dismissed by Miss Godfrey, whose family had built the large house on the corner of Manor Road. You see, they owned a good strip of the land, and refused to sell it."*

Main Street, Carlton, 1907

The old road into Carlton from Nottingham used to be called Main Street, but is now known as Carlton Hill. This photograph shows the first impression of Carlton as the traveller from Nottingham would have seen it one hundred years ago. They would have found a post office to the left, run by a Mr Tilley, and a chemist straight ahead owned by Mr Mossop. The picture below, of exactly the same view, is a far cry from this village scene. It is very odd to think that there is a period of only sixty-five years between the two photographs.

Carlton Hill, Carlton, 1972

Carlton Children's Library Rules, 1907

Note: things have changed in 100 years!

URBAN DISTRICT OF CARLTON.
Rules of the Carlton Free Lending Library
FOR CHILDREN.

Open on the evenings of Tuesdays, Thursdays, and Saturdays from 7 p.m. to 7·45 p.m.

1.—The Children of any ratepayer in the District of Carlton shall be entitled to take books out of the Library on obtaining a borrower's card, for which a charge of one penny will be made.

2.—Any child desirous of obtaining a borrower's card must have a letter of recommendation from his or her Parents or Teacher, giving full name and address, also school at which attending.

3.—Borrower's cards are not transferable.

4.—Lost cards can be replaced on payment of one penny

5.—A borrower is required to give notice to the Librarian of any change of his or her address.

6.—In applying for books a list, giving the title and number of at least six works, shall be handed to the Librarian

7.—No book will be issued unless the borrower's card is presented.

8.—No borrower shall be allowed more than one volume at the same time, and the book cannot be changed twice during the same night.

9.—The borrowers must not lend their books to any other person, and any damage to books must be reported to the Librarian.

10.—Books must not be left on the counter but must be handed to the Librarian.

11.—All books must be returned within the time specified in the covers (14 days). A fine of one penny will be charged for each fortnight for which a book is detained beyond the time allowed.

12.—The leaves of books must not be turned down or written on. If a book is lost or soiled or otherwise damaged (except by fair wear and tear) the borrower will have to replace same.

EDGAR BAKER, *Librarian*.
MAY 13th, 1907.

N.B.—The Free Library Committee respectfully ask for the co-operation of the Parents and School Teachers in carrying out these rules, and thus ensure the success of this department of the Library.

NOVEMBER, 1893.

S. Pauls, Carlton-in-the-Willows
PARISH ✝ MAGAZINE

SERVICES, NOTICES, &C.

On the First Sunday in the Month—Holy Communion 8 a.m.; Morning Prayer, Ante-Communion, Sermon and Celebration 10-45; Short Evensong and Catechizing 3-5; Baptisms 3-45; Evensong and Sermon 6-30; Choir Practise after Evensong.

The Second Sunday—Holy Communion 8 a.m.; Morning Prayer, Litany and Sermon 10-45; Children's Service, 3-5; Evensong and Sermon 6-30. Choir Practise at noon.

The Third Sunday—Holy Communion 8 a.m.; Morning Prayer and Sermon 10-45; The whole of the Holy Communion Service and Celebration (as a seperate service) at noon; Children's, Short, Service & Address 3-5; Baptisms 3-45; Evensong & Sermon 6-30; Choir Practise after Evensong.

The Fourth Sunday—Holy Communion 8 a.m.; Morning Prayer and Sermon 10-45; Choir Practise at noon; Children's Service 3-5; Evensong & Sermon 6-30.

If a Fifth Sunday—Holy Communion 8 a.m.; Morning Prayer and Sermon 10-45; Children's Service 3-5; Evensong and Sermon 6-30, followed by Short Intercession, Service for Home and Foreign Missions, with Hymns; Choir Practise at noon.

BAPTISMS—On the First and Third Sundays at 3-45, or on Wednesday Evenings at 7 o'clock, or Friday Mornings 10-30.

CHURCHINGS before or after any Service. Sunday School 9-45 and 2-30

No Fees for Baptisms or Churchings, but the offerings will be given to the Rector's Fund, for the sick and aged.

Due notice of Baptisms, Churchings, Banns and Marriages to be given to the Verger, or to the Rector, in the Vestry at the times stated, or after any service.

Verger—W. FOSTER, MAIN STREET.

Churchwardens—Mr. J. T. KNIGHT. AND Mr. WALTER DOWNES.

Clergy—Rev. E. AMYATT BURNEY, M.A., *Rector*.
Rev. J. E. FIELD, *Curate*, Station Road.

Lady Parish Worker—Miss SMITH, Brook Street.

St Paul's Parish Magazine, 1893

Foxhill Road, Carlton, 1900s

This photograph shows J. Wilkinson's horse and cart in the early 1900s on Foxhill Road. He was based at number 70 from about 1915 up until the mid-twentieth century. At some point it appears that his daughter Polly took the business over, and by the 1940s it had become known as Polly Wilko's, selling hot cobs to children for a penny on their way to school.

Floods in Vale Road, Colwick, 1910

The Trent used to flood like this every year. It would cause terrible inconvenience, as business came to a standstill and residents had to cope with the water everywhere.
Some people had it harder still: *"My grandfather used to come and stay because he'd been flooded out, and he would be a real nuisance!"*

Soldier's Homecoming, Worth Street, 1940s

This photograph shows a soldier's homecoming party at the junction of Worth Street and Foxhill Road. You can also see the wartime air raid shelters.

Overleaf: VE Day Party, Park Avenue, Carlton, 1945

Fancy Dress Parade, Deabill Street, Netherfield, 1945

Many streets celebrated the end of the war. Worth Street and Cromwell Street shared a party just like this one, with jelly, custard, and fancy dress. *"I was Mrs Mop. I remember wearing my mother's wrap-around overall, having a turban on my head and carrying a mop. We lived at the top of the street and I can remember the tables being in a long line down the street. At night there was a bonfire at the bottom of the street and someone was playing the piano accordion round the fire."*

Cavendish Road, Carlton, 1950s

Cavendish Road has a long history. It was formerly called Cemetery Lane, and before that it had been known as Stone Pit Lane since the 15th century. There was an old quarry where the Cavendish pub now stands, from which stone was taken to build All Hallows church in Gedling, the 13th century church at Strelley, and St Peter's church in Nottingham. Older still is the nearby site of a Saxon public footpath, from Sneinton to Woodborough along the bottom of Belper Avenue. This land had been donated by the lords of Caernarfon for allotments for "the poor people of Carlton in perpetuum".

Carlton Hill, 1978

"Many of Carlton's old terraced houses were eventually deemed unsafe and replaced. One summer evening an earth tremor caused a big crack in the end of the terrace on Foxhill Road. This finally made the council condemn the houses." This photograph shows similar houses, built in the eighteenth century, awaiting demolition on Carlton Hill.

Station Road, Carlton, 2005

This is a bird's eye view of Station Road which has since been obscured by the new apartments being built in the foreground. It shows the Carlton of today, with shops and houses side by side. This road is quite a busy thoroughfare to Nottingham, which is off to the left of the photograph.

Terraces on Worth Street, 1899

This old photograph shows the back yard of one of the many typical terraced houses on Worth Street. *"This was one of the main residential areas in Carlton at the turn of the century. The other main streets of the town were Beck Street, Cromwell Street, Gladstone Street and Chesterfield Street."* This house is number 20.

Carlton Post Office, c1895

In the early 1900s the post office on Cavendish Road was run by Mrs Clay. Later Mr Tilley took it over. Now the post office has moved to Station Road, and in its place is an office block.

Carlton Free Library, 1989

Carlton Free Library was officially opened on 10th February 1906 by the Right Hon J. E. Ellis, MP (although it had already been open two weeks!). Despite the atrocious weather, the whole town witnessed a grand civic parade from the old library up on Carlton Hill to the new Manor Road site where it still stands. The building cost £1800 to erect, a sum donated by the famous philanthropist Andrew Carnegie. There were 4,000 books, along with a newspaper and magazine room, a lending department, a reference department, a recreation room, and lavatory accommodation. The caretaker lived on-site, in an annexe to the left of the library which had its own kitchen and back yard, and is still used today – although no-one lives there!

Carlton Free Library, 1966

"My mother-in-law, Miss Maud Stanton, was the daughter and youngest child of John Stanton. She was born in 1889, and was issued with the first library book from the new Carlton Library in Manor Road, when it opened in 1906. By the time I was coming in the 1930s and 40s, popular books were those by Edgar Wallace, Baroness Orczy, Somerset Maughan, Dennis Wheatley, Georgette Heyer and stories about the Great War heroes." This photograph shows the old junior library.

Carlton Free Library, 1966

The long, dark wood panelling here was a feature of the old library. *"The bookcases were tall and dark, and there was a large wooden table for the children. The chief librarian was very strict, but the library assistant, Miss Welton, filled the window sills and tables with flowers from her garden.*

During the war years, there was a big target board standing outside the library, showing the amount of funds collected towards the war effort. For a few days, there was even a large bomb standing outside the front door and we children bought savings stamps and stuck them on, as we were told it was going to be dropped on Hitler!"

Carlton Free Library, 1966

Some of the library's memorable moments throughout the years range from an unidentified package which sparked a bomb scare in the 1980s, to the slow arrival of technology, hampered by the 1930s decision not to install a telephone!

Park House, 2003

Park House on Burton Road was built in 1908-09 by John Lewin of Netherfield, who was a former Liberal Councillor. It was a grand building, with stained glass from Vienna and tiles and mosaics bought direct from Italy. The building was extremely

grand, with stables, cottage, bird aviary, greenhouses, chicken coops, plus "Park Field" – an open space where Redland Avenue is now. Park House was eventually sold to the council, and then to the local area health authority on the condition that they would never sell it or use it for any purpose other than health. The building was demolished in 2003, but on its site now stands a new building used as a health clinic.

Old Police Station, 1989

The 1881 census tells us that the old Carlton police station, shown here, was on Southwell Road. By 1891, the road had changed its name to Main Street. The road is now known as Carlton Hill, and the old police station is number 88.

The Black's Head, 1975

The Black's Head was unusual in having a school use its premises. The St Paul's Church School logbook for 1869 (below) records the event. The pub itself is at least 170 years old, and possibly older.

> 5/4/69. School reassembled this day in a club-room at the Black's Head, by the direction of the Rector, — the school rooms being still engaged for the Exhibition.
> The said club-room is but a poor apology for a school-room, the benches being very awkward and cumbersome, and the access to it situated through a skittle-ground. The whole arrangement of the room was disadvanta-geous for school purposes, and the scholars were con-sequently troublesome. The attendance, however, was but small, being only 35 present at all.
> Admitted 3 new boys.

School Log Book, 1869

The Railway Hotel, 1983

When it first opened around 150 years ago, the Railway Hotel had a landlord called Jackie Bell. Colloquially the name has always been attached to the pub, and even today it is known as "Jackie Bell's". Its

attachment to the railway goes beyond the official name: an upstairs room once served as a makeshift dormitory for engine drivers and stokers visiting the large locomotive sheds nearby.

The Old Volunteer, 1975

This pub is recorded in a Carlton business directory of 1832 as "The Volunteer". The name is possibly a reference to the recruitment drive in the English Civil War, when local men signed up their service to their cause. In 1866 an inquest was held in this pub over the suspected murder of Henry Raynor at a house in Carlton. A preliminary hearing in a magistrate's court had already taken place, and the inquest here continued for two months.

The Royal Oak, 1978

This pub is now known as Inn for a Penny, having changed its name in 1984. This was another unusual pub, as there used to be monkeys in large cages in the pub garden in the late 1930s. Maybe this explains why Burton Road was known as Monkeys' Parade,

although what purpose they served is unclear! The nearby playing fields may have influenced the new name, when team players needed to quickly nip into the pub!

Royal Oak Outing in Charabanc, 1907

The word charabanc comes from the French for 'carriage with benches' (char à bancs). These vehicles resembled an open-top bus, and were common in Britain in the early twentieth century. They were especially popular for companies' annual outings to the

ROYAL OAK OUTING - 1907.

seaside, as this picture shows. Here the pub staff of the Royal Oak are on one of these trips. They cannot have been very comfortable, however, since the wheels are all solid.

Bexon's Confectioners, 1912

"Henry and Harriet Bexon had a confectioners' shop on Station Road, Carlton. This picture shows them outside their shop with their nephew Edward. The shop window contains a typical Christmas display – if you look carefully you'll see Christmas liqueurs! Henry was also the local builder and joiner, and the couple lived above the shop. Henry died in 1954 at the age of 77, outliving his wife by eighteen years."

William Widdowson, 1885

"William Widdowson was born in Carlton in 1832, and was a well-known local personality because he was the town crier – you can see his bell in the photograph. He also had a "day job", working as one of the thousands of framework knitters in the Nottinghamshire area. His wife Ann worked with him as a seamer. He died in 1907 and is buried with his wife in Carlton cemetery."

Ernie Yardley, 1940s

Ernie Yardley was an engine driver from Colwick Loco Works. The village of Netherfield grew up around the railway works located there, and many of the houses were built for railway workers.

John Leaper, c1890s

"John Leaper (1835-1914) was born in Carlton in 1835 and worked in the area all his life. This is a photograph of him working as a general carter, outside the old Windsor Castle pub. He is holding the horse's head, while the man leaning on the horse is "Stamper" Pierrepont who worked for him. His nameplate is clearly visible on the cart. In later years, he lived on Beck Street (1881), Chesterfield Street (1891), and Foxhill Road (1901), and is buried with his wife Ann in Carlton cemetery."

William Leaper, c1900s

"William Leaper (1883-1924) was a local general carter and coal merchant. He married Flora Bexon (see below) at St Paul's church on Boxing Day, 1905. At the age of 40, he had an accident with his horse and cart, after which pneumonia set in, eventually killing him. He left his widow with six children, aged between 2 and 17."

Flora Leaper, 1930s

"William's wife, Flora (1883-1964), continued to run the business, handing it over to her son William and son-in-law Harry Dring. She was often described as an angel for her generosity. When poverty was rife in the 1930s and 1940s, she would frequently give a pramful of coal to those who were too poor to afford the fuel to heat their homes."

Carlton Athletic Football Club, 1927

This photograph shows the team at their Cavendish Road ground. Some of these players' names have been lost, but on the back row, 5th and 6th from the left are Alan Wortley and Roger

Benner, and on the front row, the left-hand man is Cloggie Ward, 2nd from the left is Charlie Saxton, and 4th is "Scoffer" Peck. Among the supporters was a Mrs Etches, who was well known for attacking players of the opposing team with her umbrella if they fouled a Carlton lad. The old ground is now a cemetery.

Railway Loco Football Club, c1930s

Companies and clubs often had their own amateur teams. This one obviously drew on the railway workers from the huge works at Colwick. People on this photo include Dennis Tivey, Gordon Webb, Alf Creasey and Ernie Yardley, who donated the photograph.

Netherfield Rovers, 1943-44

"Netherfield Rovers were in the Nottingham Spartan League. Their ground was on Burton Road playing fields. Doreen Wellbourne ran the team with her mother, whilst Arthur Ibbotson used to put up the posts and nets for each home match. Some of the teams we played against were Parkmount, British Sugar Corp and Bulwell Old Boys. I had many seasons with the Rovers, firstly playing in Division One and then after winning promotion, we went up into the Premier Division in the mid 1970s. Finally, after they won the league, the team split up and the Spartan League also discontinued."

This photograph of the team on Burton Road playing fields still shows Mr Wellbourne as the manager, before Doreen took over, along with Kenny Ward, Mr Ibbotson, Bill Haywood, Mr Bennett the window-cleaner, Ron Salvin, Arthur Ibbotson, and Arthur Milns.

Netherfield Rovers Cup Presentation, 1944

The presentation was at Lawrence's Factory on Lockerbie Street.

St Paul's Cricket Team, 1937

On the back row of this photograph, from left to right are: Wilf Orchard, Veronica Shelton, Leslie Burrows, and E. Sharpe (Umpire); Middle row: two unknown gentlemen, then Neville Barlow and Andy Clarke; Front row: Len Dickinson, Albert Lipson, Rev Noble (Curate), George Fletcher, Albert Fletcher and Ernest Fletcher.

Ritz Cinema, 1978

This cinema first opened in June 1936. It was not the first cinema in Carlton, as the Victoria on Station Road had been open since April 1913 (although it is now called the Regal). The village of Netherfield, with its population of railway workers, had been first to open a cinema, however, with the Alexandra on Wright Street admitting its first customers in July 1911.

Mablethorpe Outing, 1930

WANTED

MEN OF ALL AGES

REWARD

GOOD company   .   GOOD entertainment
GOOD nights-out   .   GOOD singing

Carlton & District Male Voice Choir

COME and
👉
JOIN US!

every Monday - 7.30 p.m.
GEDLING ROAD
METHODIST
WESLEY ROOM

Carlton Male Voice Choir

"Although there is relatively little evidence of the first twenty years of the Carlton Male Voice Choir, its origins have been traced back to 1908 and the small front room of a house in Dunstan Street, Netherfield, where the coal merchant Mattie Mann and three friends gathered together to sing part songs. In the flourishing railway and mining community of the early twentieth century, more men joined them and a male voice choir was formed, drawing heavily from the local churches and chapels of the Carlton area.

"By the early 1930s, the Carlton and District Male Voice Choir was well established, holding a showpiece annual concert within Carlton, competing in and winning competitions, and travelling by train or 'saloon bus' to sing for charity at Mablethorpe and Skegness.

"The choir's activities were suspended with

the outbreak of war and challenging times lay ahead when singing resumed in peacetime. Numbers were down, sometimes barely into double figures at concerts during the 1950s. Fortunately, the choir was served by a core of determined men (two of whom were still singing well into the twenty-first century) and retained a loyal following within the local community.

"The tide turned as the 1960s heralded the start of a sustained period of progress which has continued into the new millennium. The choir adopted uniforms, initially choosing black (with gold) as its trademark colours, later replaced by the now familiar green. Ambitions were raised, with the choir singing in major venues such as Buxton Opera House, Huddersfield Town Hall and the Royal Albert Hall, holding concert tours in a number of countries in Europe and America, as well as making five commercial recordings. The current choir now draws on singers from a much wider area and approaches its centenary in 2008 in rude health and high spirits."

The Annual Concert, 1952

WESTDALE LANE
BAPTIST CHURCH
(*George Street Memorial*)

"*Week of Friendship*"

Saturday, May 17th, 1952
Commencing at 7-15 p.m.

GRAND CONCERT by

Carlton & District
Male Voice Choir
(Conductor : C. W. SANDAY)

Guest Artiste :
Kathleen G. Mitchell (*Elocutionist*)

CHAIRMAN — REV. J. DOW, H.C.F.

Stoke Bardolph Lock, 1924

"My husband learned to swim in the Trent at Stoke. By the viaduct was a little 'seaside' for people as there was a sandy bank. The river was far from clean, but one day his cousin pushed him in and he simply had to swim! After that, it became a regular occurrence to go for a swim in the Trent!" This picture shows the weir and new lock just after completion.

Cinema Listings, South Notts Echo, 1953

RITZ CARLTON CINEMA

NEXT MON., TUES., WED.

Tyrone Power
Patricia Neal and
Stephen McNally
in

DIPLOMATIC COURIER

Also (U)
PULLING STRINGS

NEXT THURS., FRI., SAT.

Johnny Weissmuller as

JUNGLE JIM IN THE FORBIDDEN LAND

(U)
Roddy McDowall, Kristine Miller
in

THE STEEL FIST

(U)

REGAL CARLTON

NEXT MON., TUES., WED.

Bing Crosby
Ingrid Bergman

in

BELLS OF ST. MARY'S

(U)

NEXT THURS., FRI., SAT.

Leo Gorcey and
The Bowery Boys
in

HERE COME THE MARINES (U)

Also

John Litel, Marie Windsor in
BEGINNERS' LUCK

(U)

COSY, NETHERFIELD

NEXT MON., TUES., WED.

Cameron Mitchell
Marguerite Chapman
in

FLIGHT TO MARS

(In Cinecolour) (U)

Leo Gorcey and the Bowery Boys
in
GHOST CHASERS (U)

NEXT THURS., FRI., SAT.

Edward G. Robinson
Lon McCallister
in

THE RED HOUSE (A)

Also

EL DORADO

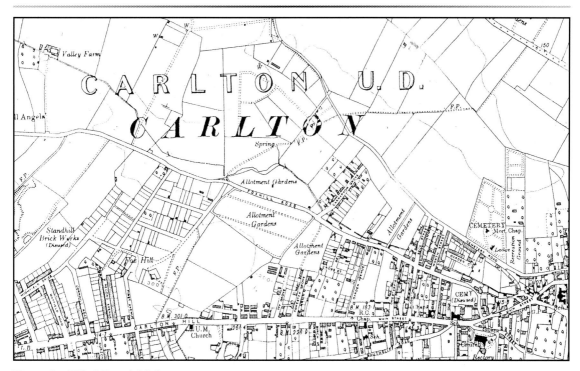

Russia Fields, 1920

This was the local play area, between Foxhill Road and Cemetery Road, shown on the map above. The name's origin is disputed: were they called "Rusher" Fields, because the water "rushed" down them when it rained? Or "Russia" because they were the highest land between Nottingham and Russia? This is how it is remembered: *"In years gone by we used to play on the Russia Fields. There were always children playing there. We would go with others and take sandwiches and a bottle of water and collect wild flowers, and take a jam jar and net to get sticklebacks from the dyke. A footpath led from Woodborough via Cavendish Road into town – it was reputedly the oldest footpath in Nottingham. It was good for you, too: Rose Leaper walked across Russia to work at the Lace Market to improve her health, as she suffered from tuberculosis."*

First tram in Carlton, 1914

"It was a real Sunday morning treat to get the tram into town from Carlton. We only got to ride on it one-way, as it cost so much money (a halfpenny each way) that we had to walk back! A man used to put salt and sand on the rails in cold weather to stop them freezing. He used to sit at the bottom of Derby Road, and we knew him as Salty Sam."

In the early 1900s, you had to walk to the Crown Inn over Carlton Hill to reach the trams. By 1912, they had reached Thorneywood Lane, and two years later the line had extended over the hill to St Paul's Church. This picture shows the very first tram to do the whole route to Carlton, on 25th June 1914.

Trolleybus, 1940

"This was the trolleybus that came up to Carlton from town: number 39. It got you to Nottingham fast." Trolleybuses proved such a hit that by 1936 they had replaced trams, only ten years after they were first introduced. The photograph shows one on Middleton Boulevard, at the peak of the trolleybus boom – at this time, the Nottingham Corporation had a fleet of 106.

Train at Colwick, 1940s

The train opened up leisure outings like never before. People could now go to the seaside for an evening, and many did. *"For two shillings and sixpence, you could leave Carlton at 5pm, get to Skegness for 8, have a couple of drinks, and then still be in time for the long journey back afterwards!"* Carlton, Netherfield and Gedling all had stations, and some people made use of the different lines to do a circular trip to Arnold and back. Here are fireman Hawthorne and driver Rowley.

Stoke Bardolph Ferry, 1900s

"For a penny, you could cross the Trent on the Stoke Bardolph ferry, landing you (and your bike) at Shelford. It was a big flat-bottomed boat, and could hold about a dozen people. A popular route was to cycle from there up to Gunthorpe, where there was a bridge, and back down the other bank of the river." The inn in this photograph is called The Ferry Boat Inn, on the Stoke side of the river. The ferryman probably worked here. It is still there today, though the ferry is no longer operational.

Radcliffe Viaduct, near Colwick, 1978

"In the early 1950s, a train crossed this old viaduct over the Trent (built in 1850 of cast iron). The crew were no doubt tired as they approached the end of their journey from Boston to Colwick. Just after they crossed the viaduct, the driver apparently realised his fireman was missing. The story goes that he was found drowned in the Trent beyond Newark, nearly 20 miles downstream."

Butcher's Advert, South Notts Echo, 1924

Colwick Sidings, c1915

The Colwick railway lines have been the scene of several nasty incidents. In 1906 the South Notts Echo ran a story headed "Decapitated at Colwick", describing how a man had been found a mile outside Colwick station. This was 33-year-old Thomas Radwin of Carlton, a plate-layer on the railway. Presumably he had been knocked down by a train, as he was lying beside the track, with his head and one hand severed from his body.

Colwick Woods, 1930

"In 1956, two trainer planes clipped their wings over Holme Pierrepont, not far from Carlton. The assembly at St John's School in Colwick heard a dreadful noise, and before they knew it, part of a wing had come down and landed in Spray and Burgess lace-dying

factory next to the school. A lady working in their canteen was killed. Parts of the plane and bodies of the pilots were later found on Nottingham race course and in Colwick woods, shown in this photograph. The engine from one of the planes actually embedded itself into the foundations of a bungalow being built at the top of Douglas Crescent. The owner, Mr Larry Gretton (a singer with the Joe Loss orchestra) reported that the impact threw him out of bed, but he was not hurt. The engine was never moved from the foundations, as it was too dangerous to do so without making the bungalow unsafe."

Shops on Carlton Hill, 1985

These shops were demolished shortly after this picture, to clear a site for a new Tesco's supermarket. But the developers got more than they bargained for. *"There used to be a graveyard and slaughterhouse on the old Tesco's site off Foxhill Road. As kids we used to play in the graveyard, digging up the old bones and playing with them. When you went down into the graves, you saw the bones where the coffins had rotted away. There was even an old willow tree whose branches looked like arms which scared everyone! When they built Tesco's on the site, which opened in 1988, the cleaner used to say she saw a ghost walking up and down. Tins of beans used to fall over at random in the middle of the night, and eventually the local vicar even went to exorcise it. One night in 1991 the whole store caught fire, which was blamed on the ghost. The manager was having none of it – all the night staff were sacked."*

Freda Beardsmore (née Leaper) was born into a well-known Carlton family. After leaving Station Road school, she worked in the Lace Market, and then at Bourne's Factory in Colwick, where Freda and her co-workers were known as Bourne's Angels. She has very fond memories of leisure activities in Carlton, being a keen dancer at the Drill Hall or the Victoria Ballroom in Nottingham. There were three cinemas to choose from: the Ritz, the Regal, and the Cosy in Netherfield. The films were changed every Thursday, so you could take your pick of the three. **Stephen Robert Brown** is related to the Leaper family and was born in Carlton. After attending St Paul's and Chandos Street schools, he became a railway plate layer at Carlton. He remembers Carlton as little more than a village, with wide open spaces at the edges where you could climb trees. **Roy Cockayne** went to Chandos Street Secondary School in Netherfield. After national service in Cyprus, he became a fireman and then an engineman at the Colwick Loco Works for nearly twenty years until it closed in 1969. **Mavis Cockayne** attended Ashwell Street and Station Road schools. **Peter Hatherley** was born in Mansfield but brought up in a three bedroomed terraced house on Foxhill Road. *"Ten of us lived there altogether: my mother,*

Above: Group photo in Carlton Library, July 2006
Below: Christine Johnson and Bernard Leaper with an old map

grandparents, aunts, uncles and sister. We had no bathroom and an outside toilet. You can imagine what bath night was like: the last one came out dirtier than when they went in! Across the road were two wash houses for our terrace to use. Coal had to be placed under the water to heat it. I remember at the side of the terraced houses was an orchard where we used to go scrumping, and by the side of it was a small field which always had a loose horse in it." **Christine Johnson** has always lived in the Carlton area and was a pupil and Pupil Teacher at St Paul's School. She taught at several schools in the Carlton and Arnold areas before becoming headteacher of Netherfield Infants' School. This meant she had to stoke the boiler when it was cold! She stayed there for 18 years. **Bernard Leaper** has many Carlton ancestors. He now lives in the old Carlton Police Station. **Margaret and Joe Smith** opened a butcher's shop at 30 Carlton Hill in 1955. Joe later became a meat inspector for Carlton Urban District Council. **Joan Spurr** owned a grocers shop in Carlton, and later ran a florists. **Doreen Richardson** grew up in Worth Street, Carlton. She went to Carlton Central and then Station Road schools. Her abiding memory is of the games she used to play in the streets, when Carlton was freer from traffic. Games like marbles, hopscotch, skipping, rounders, knock-and-run, and hide-and-seek were all safer to

Top: Roy and Mavis Cockayne looking at the library's old photograph collection
Below: Freda Beardsmore, Margaret Smith, Joe Smith, Peter Hatherley and Doreen Richardson

play in the street those days than they would be today. She worked for the Ilkeston Hosiery Company on Mar Hill Road, finishing nylon stockings in the old brewery.

Further Reading about Carlton

Barton-Ancliffe, Mel Website for St Paul's school www.ozhoo.com.au/~StPauls

Firebird Trust We've got a song: Reminiscences of Netherfield People, Firebird Trust, 1992

Heathcote, Bernard Viewing the Lifeless Body, Nottinghamshire County Council, 2005

Netherfield Local History Group Loco Village: The Birth and Growth of Netherfield, P. B. Waite, 1994

Nottinghamshire County Council Carlton: A Pictorial View, 1989

Weir, Chris As Poor as a Stockinger, Nottinghamshire County Council, 1998

Wright, Gordon The Inns and Pubs of Nottinghamshire, Nottinghamshire County Council, 1995

Acknowledgements

The compilers wish to thank all our other contributors of information and memories:

Mel Barton-Ancliffe, Don Beeston, Nellie Boardman, Alan Broadhurst, G. Brown, Jeff Buck, Andrea Davy, Chris Davis, Muriel Eyre, Gill Hunt, Ivy Kirk, Eric Lane, M. Miller, Rick Morrish, Harry Shelton, Barbara Wadd, and Pat Wagstaff.

We also gratefully acknowledge all those who have permitted us to use photographs and images as follows:

Reg Baker (p4 bottom, p11 top, p21 top, p22 top, p22 bottom, p24 top, p26 bottom, p33 top, p39 top, p40 top and bottom, p41 top, p47 bottom, p55 top, p57 top); The John Banks Collection (p53 top); Mel Barton-Ancliffe (p7 bottom); Mrs F. M. Beardsmore (p42 top and bottom, p43 bottom, p44 top); Ian Brown LRPS (p3 top, p36 top, p38 top and bottom); Mr Stephen R. Brown (p29 top); The Burton Joyce and Bulcote Local History Society Collection (p54 bottom); Carlton Male Voice Choir (p48 top and bottom, p49 top, bottom left and right); Mr R. Cockayne (p3 bottom, p17 bottom); Miss C. S. Johnson (p9 top, p9 bottom, p13 bottom, p14 bottom, p33 bottom); J. S. Johnson (p36 bottom, p37 top and bottom); Mr B. Leaper (p25 top, p44 bottom); Mrs M. Miller (p5 top); Nottingham City Council (p14 top, p50 top); Mr R. Salvin (p46 top, p46 bottom); Mrs M. Sentance (p56 bottom); Mr H. Shelton (p11 bottom, p12 top, p34, p45 top, p47 top); Marjorie Joan Spurr (p24 bottom); Mr D. Swinscoe (p25 bottom, p32 bottom); Ray Teece (p18 bottom); Trustees of the Diocese of Nottingham (p13 top); and Mrs E. S. Yardley (p19 bottom, p43 top, p45 bottom, p54 top).

We also thank Ros Brown for the photograph restoration, Tracy Dodds for the free publicity in the Nottinghamshire Family History Society Journal, and the expert team of librarians and archivists in Nottinghamshire who have helped with the research. Finally we acknowledge the invaluable work of Rupert Vinnicombe and Mark Dorrington, who oversaw the whole project.